JUN 1 0 2014

D0844338

ROCKS: The Hard Facts

MINERALS

Willa Dee

Indian Prairie Public Library District
401 Plainfield Road ~ Darien, IL 60561

PowerKiDS press™

New York

Published in 2014 by The Rosen Publishing Group, Inc.
29 East 21st Street, New York, NY 10010

First Edition

Editor: Jennifer Way
Book Design: Kate Vlachos
Photo Research: Katie Stryker

Photo Credits: Cover, p. 14 (right) Joel Arem/Photo Researchers/Getty Images; p. 4 Tom Grundy/Shutterstock.com; p. 5 In Green/Shutterstock.com; p. 6 Africa Studio/Shutterstock.com; p. 7 (left) Rob Lavinsky/Wikimedia Commons/File:Carletonite-250275.jpg; p. 7 (right) Marcel Jancovic/Shutterstock.com; p. 8 (left) Biophoto Associates/Photo Researchers/Getty Images; p. 8 (right) Mark A. Schneider/Photo Researchers/Getty Images; p. 9 Morgenstjerne/Shutterstock.com; p. 10 Science Source/Photo Researchers/Getty Images; p. 11 (left) Steve Gschmeissner/Science Photo Library/Getty Images; p. 11 (right) Jubal Harshaw/Shutterstock.com; p. 12 (left) DEA/R. Appiani/De Agostini Picture Library/Getty Images; p. 12 (right) mykeyruna/Shutterstock.com; p. 13 koi88/Shutterstock.com; p. 14 (left) Steve Estvanik/Shutterstock.com; p. 16 (left) Imfoto/Shutterstock.com; p. 16 (right) AVprophoto/Shutterstock.com; p. 17 Jane Rix/Shutterstock.com; p. 18 claffra/Shutterstock.com; p. 19 Dr. Marli Miller/Visuals Unlimited/Getty Images; p. 20 optimarc/Shutterstock.com; p. 21 M. Khebra/Shutterstock.com; p. 22 Maggie Molloy/Shutterstock.com.

Publisher's Cataloguing Data

Dee, Willa. Minerals / by Willa Dee.
  p. cm. — (Rocks: the hard facts)
Includes index.
ISBN 978-1-4777-2905-2 (library binding) — ISBN 978-1-4777-2994-6 (pbk.) — ISBN 978-1-4777-3064-5 (6-pack)
1. Minerals — Juvenile literature. 2. Mineralogy — Juvenile literature. I. Title.
QE363.8 D44 2014
549—dc23

Manufactured in the United States of America

CPSIA Compliance Information: Batch #W14PK4: For Further Information contact Rosen Publishing, New York, New York at 1-800-237-9932

CONTENTS

WHAT ARE MINERALS?

Geology is the study of Earth's **physical** history. Scientists who study geology are called geologists. Today, geologists look at Earth's rocks to learn more about Earth's past.

Geologists have found that Earth's rocks are made up of minerals. Minerals are **solid** substances found naturally on Earth. People do not make them, and they are not made from living things.

This geologist is studying Earth's rocks and minerals. The study of rocks is called geology, and the study of minerals is called mineralogy.

Not all rocks are made up of only minerals. Some rocks, like this chalk, are made up of the remains of dead plants or animals.

While many minerals are found in rocks, minerals can also be found on their own. Together, rocks and minerals make up Earth's crust. The crust is Earth's hard outer layer. Geologists have **identified** about 4,000 minerals on Earth so far.

Minerals are made up of substances called elements. Elements are the basic matter from which all things on Earth are made. Tiny particles called atoms form elements. Each element is made up of just one kind of atom.

Gold is a mineral made up of only one element. That means that it cannot be broken down into any smaller parts.

Minerals can be made up of any number of elements. Carletonite (left) is made up of eight elements. Aragonite (right) is made up of three elements. They are calcium, carbon, and oxygen.

There are more than 100 elements on Earth. Different elements form different minerals. Some minerals are compounds. Compounds are made up of more than one element. Other minerals are made up of just one element.

The combination of elements that forms a certain mineral will always form that mineral. This is a mineral's **chemical** makeup.

WHAT ARE CRYSTALS?

Minerals form through a process called crystallization. Crystallization starts with the atoms that make up the elements in the mineral. First, these atoms stack up in a pattern. Then, the pattern repeats itself over and over.

The minerals diamond (left) and graphite (right) are both made up of the element carbon. They look different because they have different crystal structures.

Amethyst is the purple variety of the mineral quartz. It is made up of the elements silicon and oxygen.

This forms a solid object called a crystal. Crystals have flat sides that meet at different **angles** to form sharp edges.

Crystals come in many different shapes and sizes. A crystal's shape depends on the number of sides it has. It also depends on what kind of angles form the crystal's edges. The shape a crystal forms is called the mineral's crystal **structure**. Every mineral has its own crystal structure.

IDENTIFYING MINERALS

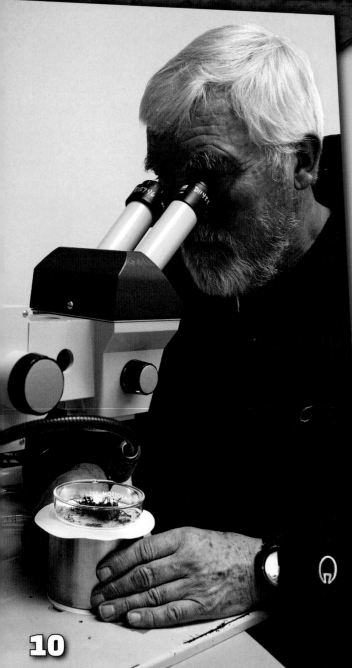

Every mineral has a set of physical features, or properties. These properties help geologists identify a mineral, or tell it apart from other minerals. A mineral's crystal structure is one of its physical properties. Geologists often look at a mineral's crystals with a **microscope** or an **X-ray**.

This scientist is looking at a mineral under a microscope. The microscope will let him see the mineral up close so that he can identify the mineral's crystal structure.

Above left: This picture shows what one phosphate crystal looks like under a microscope. All phosphate minerals have the elements phosphorus and oxygen in them. *Right*: Scientists use a special kind of light to see more parts of minerals. The picture on the top is of the mineral serpentine in regular light. The picture on the bottom is of the same mineral in that special light.

Some physical properties of minerals can be seen with just your eyes. A mineral's color is one of these physical properties. To **observe** other physical properties, you will need to perform tests on a mineral sample. The results of the tests will help you figure out the sample's identity.

PROPERTIES YOU CAN SEE

You can observe a mineral's color just by looking at it. However, many minerals come in different colors. This means that two samples of the same mineral may not be the same color! Other minerals are nearly always the same color. A mineral's color also can be metallic or nonmetallic. Minerals may also have layers, streaks, or spots of colors.

The mineral quartz can be many different colors. This chrysoprase (left) is blue green, and this rose quartz (right) is pink.

Pyrite is a mineral with metallic luster. Pyrite is commonly called fool's gold because it looks so much like the element gold.

Luster is another **visible** physical property. Luster is the measure of how well the surface of a mineral **reflects** light. Minerals with metallic luster reflect a lot of light, as metals do. Minerals with nonmetallic luster still reflect light, but they are not as shiny.

TESTING AND OBSERVING

Many physical properties of minerals can be observed only through testing. Scratching is a test that shows how hard a mineral is. Some soft minerals, such as talc, can be scratched with just your fingernail. Other minerals are very hard. Diamonds are so hard that only other diamonds can scratch them.

Below left: You also can test how minerals break apart. Obsidian shows a property called fracture because it splits along a rough, irregular surface. Some minerals break along a flat, smooth surface. *Below right*: Some minerals, like malachite (right), have the same streak color as they do body color. Other minerals, like hematite (left), have different streak and body colors.

Mohs' Hardness Scale

Mineral	Mohs' Hardness Scale	Approximate Hardness of Common Objects
Talc	1	
Gypsum	2	Fingernail (2.5)
Calcite	3	Copper penny (3.5)
Fluorite	4	Iron nail (4.5)
Apatite	5	Glass (5.5)
Feldspar	6	Steel file (6.5)
Quartz	7	Streak plate (7.0)
Topaz	8	
Corundum	9	
Diamond	10	

Geologists use a scale, called the Mohs' scale, to rank the hardness of minerals. The Mohs' scale ranks 10 common minerals from softest to hardest.

Streak is the measure of a mineral's color in its powdered form. You can observe streak by scraping a mineral against a tile called a streak plate. Transparency is the measure of how much light passes through a mineral. You can observe transparency by cutting a thin slice of the mineral and holding it to the light.

Above left: This picture shows the mineral beryl. Green beryl crystals are cut and polished into emerald gemstones. *Above right*: These are diamond earrings. Because diamonds are a rare, or hard to find, mineral, diamond jewelry is very expensive.

All minerals are made up of crystals. However, some minerals form crystals that are rare and beautiful. When these minerals are cut and polished, they are called gemstones. Gemstones are often used in expensive **jewelry**.

Some gemstones are also known as birthstones. Every month of the year has its own birthstone. People have been wearing their birthstones in pieces of jewelry for hundreds of years!

Diamonds are minerals made of carbon atoms. When diamonds are cut and polished, they become very sparkly. The mineral corundum can form two different kinds of gemstones. When corundum mixes with the element chromium, its cut and polished crystals are called rubies. When corundum mixes with elements such as iron, copper, or magnesium, its crystals can be cut and polished into sapphires.

Birthstones

Month		Stone
January		Garnet
February		Amethyst
March		Aquamarine
April		Diamond
May		Emerald
June		Pearl
July		Ruby
August		Peridot
September		Sapphire
October		Opal
November		Topaz
December		Turquoise

SILICATE MINERALS

Minerals are grouped into classes. The most common class of minerals is silicate minerals. Because most rocks are made up of silicate minerals, silicate minerals form most of Earth's crust. All silicate minerals contain the elements silicon and oxygen. Other common elements in silicate minerals include aluminum, magnesium, iron, calcium, sodium, and potassium.

This picture shows lightly colored quartz surrounded by darker granite rocks. Together, quartz and granite make up this part of Earth's crust in Norway.

This part of Earth's crust is made up of metamorphic and igneous rocks and the minerals quartz and feldspar. Feldspar is often found in metamorphic and igneous rocks.

Quartz is a common silicate mineral. Quartz crystals are formed from a pattern of silicon and oxygen atoms. Quartz is often colorless and transparent, although it can also come in many different colors. Quartz is often used in jewelry. Together with feldspar, another silicate mineral, quartz forms much of Earth's **continental crust**.

NONSILICATE MINERALS

All other mineral classes form a group called nonsilicate minerals. Nonsilicate minerals make up less than 10 percent of Earth's crust.

There are several kinds of nonsilicate minerals. Native elements are minerals that are formed from just one element. This mineral class includes gold, silver, and copper. Sulfides are a mineral class that includes many metal ores.

Gold is a native element. Most elements are silver or white, but gold is yellow. Gold's color is one of the reasons why it is popular.

This picture shows the metal ore iron. Iron ore is often made up of the elements iron, oxygen, hydrogen, and carbon.

Metal ores are minerals from which metals can be **extracted.** Sulfate minerals are formed from the element sulfate combined with oxygen and other elements. Gypsum is a sulfate mineral commonly used in building construction.

PART OF THE CYCLE

All rocks are made up of minerals. Minerals make up Earth's three kinds of rock, which are sedimentary rock, igneous rock, and metamorphic rock.

Minerals play an important part in the rock cycle. The rock cycle is Earth's process of breaking down existing rocks and forming new rocks. Sometimes the minerals are unchanged when they become part of a new rock. Other times great heat and pressure can cause a mineral to change as a new rock forms. Earth's rock cycle is a slow process that goes on forever.

Granite is an igneous rock. It is mainly made up of the minerals quartz and feldspar.

GLOSSARY

angles (ANG-gulz) The spaces between lines or planes that come together at a point.

chemical (KEH-mih-kul) Matter that can be mixed with other matter to cause changes.

continental crust (kon-tuh-NEN-tul KRUST) The moving pieces of Earth's outermost layer.

extracted (ek-STRAKT-ed) To have taken one item out of another.

identified (eye-DEN-tuh-fyd) Figured out what something is.

jewelry (JOO-ul-ree) Objects worn for decoration that are made of special metals, such as gold and silver, and prized stones.

microscope (MY-kruh-skohp) An instrument used to see very small things.

observe (ub-ZERV) To notice.

physical (FIH-zih-kul) Having to do with natural forces.

reflects (rih-FLEKTS) Throws back light, heat, or sound.

solid (SOH-led) Matter that is hard.

structure (STRUK-cher) Form.

visible (VIH-zih-bul) Able to be seen.

X-ray (EKS-ray) A special picture that can be taken of the inside of something.

INDEX

WEBSITES

Due to the changing nature of Internet links, PowerKids Press has developed an online list of websites related to the subject of this book. This site is updated regularly. Please use this link to access the list:
www.powerkidslinks.com/rthf/miner/